The earth is the LORD's and all that is in it,
the world, and those who live in it.
- Psalm 24

A MILLION PRAYERS

PRAYERS

TO SOLVE OUR CLIMATE CRISIS

Dedications

For God, our loving Father and Creator, and Christ our Savior. We need you. Please give us faith to pray and courage to act.

For our children and generations of unborn children. They have no choice but to live with the earth that we pass to them. May we leave it looking more like God's creation.

For you, the reader, and for everyone who is willing to pray and act to solve our climate crisis. Proceeds from this book will support you through MillionPrayerMission.org.

Contents

Introduction   1

This book is a prayer for a million prayers.

Chapter 1   6

God created everything. He made the earth, and he made us.

Chapter 2   25

God gave us minds for science, so good science honors God.

Chapter 3   34

Good science tells us that God's earth has a fever, and it's getting worse every year.

Chapter 4   54

Christians are called to solve climate change, and we need God's help.

Chapter 5   68

Let's pray, act, and pray again.

Acknowledgments   77

Author's Note   80

Introduction

This book is a prayer
for a million prayers.

If you were to ask God for a million prayers, for whom or for what would you pray?

I am praying for God's help to solve climate change, a problem that affects all of us. Yes, climate change is real. Please see Chapter 3 for the facts.

In all of human history, our climate has never changed this quickly. The impacts are all around us, and they are going to get worse before they get better. Unfortunately, we are not prepared.

We, our children, and generations of unborn children face greater risk with every passing year that we fail to find a solution to climate change. That's why this is "our climate crisis." I'm asking for your prayers, and a million others, to help solve it.

Who am I to ask for a million prayers?

Who am I to ask God to help us solve climate change? I'm not a pastor or a prophet. I don't have a Ph.D. in theology or climate science, and I don't have a million followers on social media.

But I am a Christian. I'm also a parent. As such, I believe that I have a duty to pray and act to solve climate change.

As a Christian, I love God, and I believe *"God so loved the world that he gave his only Son, so that whoever believes in him shall not perish but have eternal life"* (John 3:16). Our Creator is all-powerful. He spoke the universe into motion. He created the earth. He created every living thing, including us. He made us in his own image and gave us a sacred responsibility: to be the keepers of his creation. This is an essential element of our Christian faith that we seem to have forgotten, and God is now redirecting our attention.

As a parent, I love my kids dearly. They are each made in God's image, and I hope to see them in heaven one day. Until then, they deserve to live out their days on a planet that is as good as God intended. Their children deserve that too, and so do their children's children. When my kids are old enough to understand the gravity of climate change, I want to look into their eyes and tell them, "I did everything I could to prepare a better life for you."

Thankfully, I am not alone. *You* are reading this book, and you're invited to be part of a rapidly growing circle of prayer and action to solve climate change.

Welcome to the Million Prayer Mission.

Jesus encourages us to ask God for what we need: "*So I tell you, whatever you ask for in prayer, believe that you have received it, and it will be yours*" (Mark 11:24). As Christians, we believe that God answers prayers—according to his will and in proportion to our faith.

That's why we launched the Million Prayer Mission. We are asking for God's help to solve climate change, and there are opportunities to pray throughout this book. Please post your prayers online and invite others to do the same at MillionPrayerMission.org.

Why a million prayers? It's not a magic number. It's a goal to help us elevate our prayers to the level of the climate crisis. The Creator of heaven and earth doesn't need a single prayer to solve climate change. He is God. He could solve it with a mere thought or whisper. However, God made us to be the keepers of his creation, and I believe he wants to see us taking that responsibility seriously. A million prayers to solve climate change would be an offering of good faith—a chance to show God that we care about his earth and his people.

What about action? Throughout the Gospels, Jesus emphasizes that our actions matter as much as our words. For instance, *"Not everyone who says to me, 'Lord, Lord,' will enter the kingdom of heaven, but only the one who does the will of my Father in heaven"* (Matthew 7:21).

As Christians, we believe in the power of prayer *and* action. This book calls for both.

Step into the story.

Five chapters explain why Christians are called to help solve climate change, and how we can turn back the tide.

- Chapter 1: God created everything. He made the earth, and he made us.
- Chapter 2: God gave us minds for science, so good science honors God.
- Chapter 3: Good science tells us that God's earth has a fever, and it's getting worse every year.
- Chapter 4: Christians are called to solve climate change, and we need God's help.
- Chapter 5: Let's pray, act, and pray again.

I wrote this book because we are living in a moment of profound consequence. Generations of God's people depend on what we do next.

At times, we may doubt whether we can make a meaningful difference with a problem as big as climate change. It's bigger than any one of us. Yet our Savior encourages us to have faith:

> *Truly I tell you, if you have faith as small*
> *as a mustard seed, you can say to this mountain,*
> *'Move from here to there,' and it will move.*
> *Nothing will be impossible for you.*
> - Matthew 17:20

This is where you and your faith step into the story.

Chapter 1

God created everything.
He made the earth, and he made us.

God created *everything.*

This is a simple statement of faith, and it's also an amazing statement. It's at the foundation of the Holy Bible, our Christian faith, and even our relationship with God.

How do we know that? Because it's in the Bible—the first book, first chapter, and first sentence: *"In the beginning when God created the heavens and the earth…"* (Genesis 1:1).

With these first few words, we learn that God is our infinite and all-powerful Creator. God spoke the universe into motion. He made all of the stars, including the sun. He made all of the planets, including the earth. Then he made every living thing on earth, including us.

In the midst of all this creativity, one truth stands out: Whatever God creates belongs to God. We'll revisit this truth in the pages ahead. For now, let's dive deeper into Genesis.

As the first chapter of the Bible, Genesis 1 can be easy to take for granted. Many of us first heard the creation story when we were kids and never looked back. Or maybe we have heard the story so many times that it no longer captivates our imagination. Here is an opportunity to explore Genesis 1 with new eyes.

As we walk through the "days of creation," we'll focus on significant actions taken by our Creator: *God made, God said, God called, God blessed, God saw that it was good,* and *God rested.* After each scripture passage, we'll reflect on our heavenly Father's actions and what they say about his character, the value of his creation, and his boundless love for each of us.

Day 1. Genesis 1:1-5

1 In the beginning when God created the heavens and the earth,
2 the earth was a formless void and darkness covered the face of the deep, while a wind from God swept over the face of the waters.
3 Then God said, "Let there be light," and there was light.
4 And God saw that the light was good; and God separated the light from the darkness.

⁵ God called the light Day, and the darkness he called Night. And there was evening and there was morning, the first day.

To say that God took action on Day 1 is an understatement. This may have been the most action-packed day in history! Let's pause here to reflect on the meaning of two major actions: *"God created"* and *"God said."*

Why does God create?

God creates because he is *great*. He makes the biggest and smallest things, and he makes them with incredible complexity and abundance. We can even see God's greatness within us. *"I praise you, for I am fearfully and wonderfully made. Wonderful are your works; that I know very well"* (Psalm 139:14).

God creates because he is an *artist*. He loves beauty of all kinds. God doesn't just hang one painting, of one color, inside one art gallery. He completely immerses us in his art. His creation is made with every possible color and substance. He wants us to experience it with all of our senses. In fact, we are all part of God's creation, and we each have a special role to play in his masterpiece.

God creates because he is *generous*. He has given us life itself. He has given us everything we need to live. Knowing how much we value our short lives on earth, God even offers us a chance to live forever. Could any gift be more generous?

God creates because he *loves* us. We are God's children, and he is our loving Father. All of the greatness, beauty, and generosity of God's works are expressions of his love. His creation is a lasting reminder that he is with each of us, and he is for us.

God said, "Let there be light."

What may have happened in this moment? God didn't just speak four words. He launched our entire universe. His voice is still reverberating across it, extending the boundaries of space and time.

How big is the universe? *At least* 27.6 billion light-years across. And that's just the "observable universe" that we can measure with a telescope. What does this mean? Assuming we could travel at the speed of light, and we had the time, it would take us 27.6 billion years to fly across the entire observable universe!

Then we would need to keep going, because God's universe is bigger than we can see with a telescope, and it's expanding.[1] Astronomers have discovered that distant

---

[1] space.com/33306-how-does-the-universe-expand-faster-than-light.html

galaxies are moving rapidly away from us and away from each other. It's like when a firework explodes in the sky and sends sparks flying in every direction. In the same way, the path of every object in the universe can be traced back to one great explosion: *"Let there be light."*

Everything in existence points us back to God.

Day 2. Genesis 1:6-8

6 And God said, "Let there be a dome in the midst of the waters, and let it separate the waters from the waters."
7 So God made the dome and separated the waters that were under the dome from the waters that were above the dome. And it was so.
8 God called the dome Sky. And there was evening and there was morning, the second day.

In the passage above, God named the Sky, just as he named Day, Night, Earth, and Sea in other passages.

There is power in naming. To name something is the prerogative of its creator—the stamp of its owner. An artist names his art because it's his unique work. For example, Leonardo Da Vinci painted and named the *Mona Lisa*. No matter who possesses the painting today, it will always be Da Vinci's *Mona Lisa*. In the same way, God's creation will always belong to God.

A name also gives value and purpose. When God made the atmosphere and called it *"Sky,"* he did it for a reason. In Chapter 3, we will explore the essential role that our atmosphere plays in God's creation.

Day 3. Genesis 1:9-13

9 And God said, "Let the waters under the sky be gathered together into one place, and let the dry land appear." And it was so.

10 God called the dry land Earth, and the waters that were gathered together he called Seas. And God saw that it was good.

11 Then God said, "Let the earth put forth vegetation: plants yielding seed, and fruit trees of every kind on earth that bear fruit with the seed in it." And it was so.

12 The earth brought forth vegetation: plants yielding seed of every kind, and trees of every kind bearing fruit with the seed in it. And God saw that it was good.

13 And there was evening and there was morning, the third day.

What does it mean when the Bible says, *"God saw that it was good"*?

Did God only make a passive observation of his creation's goodness? Suppose he finished making the earth, looked at it, and was surprised to find that it turned out to be good. If that were the case, God's creation would just be a fortunate accident.

But God doesn't create accidents. He creates with purpose. His words and actions are never wasted. Therefore, *"God saw that it was good"* is not a passive observation. It is an intentional action—an act of divine will. God not only *saw*, but he also saw *to it* that his earth was good.

The inherent goodness of God's earth raises an important question: How should we respond when the earth's goodness is at risk?

Day 4. Genesis 1:14-19

14 And God said, "Let there be lights in the dome of the sky to separate the day from the night; and let them be for signs and for seasons and for days and years,
15 and let them be lights in the dome of the sky to give light upon the earth." And it was so.
16 God made the two great lights—the greater light to rule the day and the lesser light to rule the night—and the stars.
17 God set them in the dome of the sky to give light upon the earth,
18 to rule over the day and over the night, and to separate the light from the darkness. And God saw that it was good.
19 And there was evening and there was morning, the

fourth day.

On Day 1, God said, *"Let there be light,"* and on Day 4 he said, *"Let there be lights"*—plural.

He wound up the earth like a great clock, and then he sent it spinning in circles around the sun. God established the rhythms of the moon and stars. With all of these celestial bodies working together in predictable patterns, we can now count the passage of days, months, seasons, and years.

God created time as we know it.

Day 5. Genesis 1:20-23

[20] And God said, "Let the waters bring forth swarms of living creatures, and let birds fly above the earth across the dome of the sky."
[21] So God created the great sea monsters and every living creature that moves, of every kind, with which the waters swarm, and every winged bird of every kind. And God saw that it was good.
[22] God blessed them, saying, "Be fruitful and multiply and fill the waters in the seas, and let birds multiply on the earth."
[23] And there was evening and there was morning, the fifth day.

We just witnessed God's first blessing in the Bible. It was a surprising moment because God gave his blessing to some unlikely recipients: *"every living creature,"* including fish and birds.

As humans, we think of ourselves as first in God's eyes. Of course, we don't have to wait too long for our blessing in Genesis 1:28, just six lines later. Even so, we are not the first in line. This is a good time to step back and humbly ask two questions: What is a blessing, and why did God bless every living creature before us?

Merriam-Webster defines the verb "bless" as follows: to hallow or consecrate by religious rite or word, invoke divine care for, praise, glorify, speak well of, approve, confer prosperity or happiness upon, protect, preserve, endow, or favor.[2]

Those are valid definitions, yet there may be one missing: love. To bless is to love. When we pray, we often ask God to bless our loved ones. Parents bless their children. In the same way, God blesses what and whom he loves.

As we can see, a blessing is more than just a word. Before we settle on one definition, let's look to the language in which Genesis was first written: ancient Hebrew. The Hebrew root of the verb "bless" is *barak*, which means "to kneel." In the context of Genesis 1:22, the Hebrew means "to bend the knee

---

[2] merriam-webster.com/dictionary/bless

to present a gift."[3]

When God gives his blessing to every living creature, we can imagine him bending a knee to present a gift. And what is God's gift? Life itself. He says, *"Be fruitful and multiply and fill the waters in the seas, and let birds multiply on the earth."* God gives life to every creature, and to continue that gift, he gives them the ability to reproduce.

Now that we know what a blessing is, we can address our second question: *Why did God bless every living creature before us?*

To offer a simplistic answer, we know that humans were not even in the picture on Day 5, so how could God bless us first? God didn't just *bless* every living creature before us; he *created* everything else before us.

Why? One possible explanation: God created everything before us because he wanted to lay a strong foundation for our lives on earth. Each step along the path of creation leads to more complex forms of life. Without the building blocks of life from Days 1 through 5, we could not survive.

Beyond mere necessity, life without the rest of God's creation would be much less diverse, beautiful, and interesting. Imagine earth without any plants or animals. God made them

------

[3] ancient-hebrew.org/living-words/the-living-words-bless.htm

first because he knew that the rest of creation would make our lives better.

Last but not least, God was leading by example when he blessed every living creature first. If God gives them great respect, then shouldn't we? If God bends a knee to give his creatures the gift of life, then shouldn't we?

Day 6. Genesis 1:24-31

[24] And God said, "Let the earth bring forth living creatures of every kind: cattle and creeping things and wild animals of the earth of every kind." And it was so.
[25] God made the wild animals of the earth of every kind, and the cattle of every kind, and everything that creeps upon the ground of every kind. And God saw that it was good.
[26] Then God said, "Let us make humankind in our image, according to our likeness; and let them have dominion over the fish of the sea, and over the birds of the air, and over the cattle, and over all the wild animals of the earth, and over every creeping thing that creeps upon the earth."
[27] So God created humankind in his image, in the image of God he created them; male and female he created them.
[28] God blessed them, and God said to them, "Be fruitful and multiply, and fill the earth and subdue it; and have

dominion over the fish of the sea and over the birds of the air and over every living thing that moves upon the earth."

29 God said, "See, I have given you every plant yielding seed that is upon the face of all the earth, and every tree with seed in its fruit; you shall have them for food.

30 And to every beast of the earth, and to every bird of the air, and to everything that creeps on the earth, everything that has the breath of life, I have given every green plant for food." And it was so.

31 God saw everything that he had made, and indeed, it was very good. And there was evening and there was morning, the sixth day.

Day 6 is important because God created us and set us apart for a special role on earth.

Genesis 1:26-27 states four times that we are made in God's *"image"* or *"likeness."* On the surface, these words suggest that we might be made to look like God in our physical appearance. However, the Bible's ancient Hebrew translation offers a deeper meaning. The Hebrew word for "image" is *tselem*, which literally means "shadow" or "representation."[4]

Tselem also refers to our purpose. When God made us in his image and likeness, he also gave us our purpose: to be like

_____

[4] ancient-hebrew.org/god-yhwh/the-image-of-god.htm

him and to represent him on earth.

Next, how are we to understand God's blessing in Genesis 1:28? Just as God blessed every living creature on Day 5, he blessed us on Day 6. He said, *"Be fruitful and multiply, and fill the earth…"*

Then he said something very different. With the word *"subdue,"* God acknowledged us as the dominant species on the planet. With the words *"have dominion"* —or *"rule over"* in some translations—God put us in charge of his earth. In doing so, he gave us a sacred responsibility as the earth's keepers, or stewards.

The Bible tells us that God expects a lot from his stewards. As Jesus said, *"From everyone to whom much has been given, much will be required; and from the one to whom much has been entrusted, even more will be demanded"* (Luke 12:48).

No matter how much dominion or authority we might assume for ourselves as stewards, we need to remember that God created the earth, and the earth is God's: *"The earth is the LORD's and all that is in it, the world, and those who live in it"* (Psalm 24).

Our treatment of God's earth and God's people reflects our relationship with God.

Day 7. Genesis 2:1-3

1 Thus the heavens and the earth were finished, and all their multitude.
2 And on the seventh day God finished the work that he had done, and he rested on the seventh day from all the work that he had done.
3 So God blessed the seventh day and hallowed it, because on it God rested from all the work that he had done in creation.

This is the first Sabbath, or Shabbat in Hebrew. It's significant not because of what God *did*, but because of what he *didn't* do.

Based on Genesis and the Ten Commandments, Jewish people have observed the Sabbath for thousands of years on the seventh day of the week. As a Jew, Jesus did too. Today, most Christians observe the Sabbath on the first day of the week, in honor of Jesus' resurrection day. Either way, the principle is the same: We all need to rest. If God took a day off, so can we.

The Sabbath is a holy day set aside for us by God. It's an opportunity to step back from our work to appreciate and enjoy all that God has already done.

God's continuous creation

God's creation is a divine process. As we just read, the Book of Genesis tells the story over the course of seven days. Did God stop creating after that? Of course not. God is alive, and he continues to shape his creation and our lives as well.

God is still creating through nature. Just walk outside and look for signs of God-given life: a budding tree or a singing bird.

God is still creating through us. Every day, about 400,000 babies are born,[5] and every one of them has a unique ability to contribute to God's creation and build up God's kingdom on earth.

My five-year-old daughter, Rachel, put it this way: "God is the best! He made everything. He is still making things, and he helps us to make things too." It's so true that even a five-year-old knows it. As a case in point, at the time of this quote Rachel was producing several works of art each day, and we nearly ran out of places to put them.

Clearly, the evidence of God's continuous creativity is all around us, and within each of us.

---

[5] unicef.org/press-releases/new-years-babies-over-395000-children-will-be-born-worldwide-new-years-day-unicef

Gratitude for every good thing

How can we even begin to thank God for his all-encompassing creation? What can we offer in return for the gift of life?

Let's begin by thanking and praising God.

While we sing God's praises, let's also remember that we are in good company. As the Bible says, "*all the earth*" joins us in making a joyful noise for our King and Creator (Psalm 98).

That is just what God intended, because he is behind it all:

God is behind the hopeful "good morning" of a sunrise, and also the brilliant glowing "goodbye" of a sunset.

God is behind the sights, sounds, and smells of the ocean; a coral reef teeming with life in every color of the rainbow; the ceaseless tides; and the waves pounding the coast.

God is behind a soaring eagle and a million migratory birds filling the sky with flapping wings.

God is behind towering mountains covered in a fresh blanket of snow; waterfalls; a peaceful river meandering through a verdant valley; and the wind rustling over a forest canopy as hundreds of tree trunks creak in unison.

God is behind the stark simplicity of the desert; a starry night; a flash of lightning; a peal of thunder; and the smell of rain after the storm.

God is in the place we call home; the people we love; and the look in a loved one's eyes that says, "No matter what, I love you."

Every good thing comes from God, so it all points back *to* God. And it always has, since the moment of *"Let there be light."*

Make a joyful noise to the LORD, all the earth;
break forth into joyous song and sing praises.
Sing praises to the LORD with the lyre,
with the lyre and the sound of melody.
With trumpets and the sound of the horn
make a joyful noise before the King, the LORD.
Let the sea roar, and all that fills it;
the world and those who live in it.
Let the floods clap their hands;
let the hills sing together for joy
at the presence of the LORD, for he is coming
to judge the earth.
He will judge the world with righteousness,
and the peoples with equity.
- Psalm 98

Prayer Challenge

Let's give thanks to our Creator for making the earth and making each of us.

How has God blessed your life with his greatness, beauty, generosity, and love?

_____

_____

_____

_____

_____

_____

_____

_____

_____

To add your prayer to the Million Prayer Mission,
please visit MillionPrayerMission.org.

Chapter 2

God gave us minds for science, so good science honors God.

In the last chapter, we explored how God created the earth and how God created us.

In this chapter, we will focus on our God-given minds and how they help us to understand and appreciate God's creation.

For thousands of years, people have known about the importance of the mind. So did Jesus. When asked which was the first of God's commandments, Jesus answered, *"The first is, 'Hear, O Israel: the Lord our God, the Lord is one; you shall love the Lord your God with all your heart, and with all your soul, and with all your mind, and with all your strength'"* (Mark 12:29-30).

Not everyone knows that Jesus added the phrase, *"with all your mind,"* to the original Hebrew verse from Deuteronomy 6:5. The original verse reads: *"You shall love the LORD your God with all your heart, and with all your soul, and with all your might."*

Why did Jesus add *"with all your mind"* to this commandment? Let's take a closer look.

The ancient Greek word for "mind" is *dianoia,*[6] which is the word used throughout the New Testament. While it is sometimes translated as "mind," "thought," or "understanding," the ancient Greek origin of the word reveals even more meaning. The prefix *dia-* means "all the way across and through," and *-noia* refers to "the mind."

Over three hundred years before Jesus walked the earth, the Greek philosopher Plato popularized the word *dianoia.* Plato was the founder of the first-ever university, and he used *dianoia* to describe a method of critical thinking to solve scientific problems.[7] Another *dia-* word, *diameter,* gives us a helpful analogy. A diameter is a line that goes all the way across and through the center of a circle. In the same way, Plato encouraged his students to think through scientific problems from all sides or viewpoints as they worked together to find a solution.

---

[6] biblehub.com/greek/1271.htm
[7] en.wikipedia.org/wiki/Dianoia

So, why did Jesus command us to love God with all our minds? Because God wants us to love him—all the way across and through our minds. He wants us to consider different viewpoints, use our critical thinking skills, and work together to solve problems. God places a high value on our minds, as well as our hearts, souls, and strength.

God gave us curious minds for a reason.

God hardwired our minds to ask complex questions about the world around us.

For example, our ancestors might have asked, "Why does this edible plant grow here but not there? Why does it grow only during the warmer months? How can we grow more of it?" By asking questions like these and seeking answers, we eventually learned how to farm, which was the foundation of civilization.

Asking and answering questions is a natural part of being human, and we continue to ask questions every day. It typically works like this: We ask a question, and then we take our best guess at an answer. Next, we make observations to see if our guess is correct. If not, we guess again, and observe again, until we find the answer.

This process of trial and error is basically *science*.

Science is a disciplined approach to asking and answering questions about the physical world around us. It allows us to do amazing things: treat diseases, walk on the moon, communicate instantly across vast distances, and so much more. It also helps us to understand the great complexity and abundance of God's creation. The knowledge that we gain from science reinforces the miracle of life on earth and the value of everything made by God.

If God gave us minds for science, then *good* science honors God.

What is good science?

First, good science is *ethical*. Let's consider one type of scientist, a doctor. The reason we go to a doctor is to be healed, and every good doctor follows the ethical principle of "First, do no harm." The same principle applies to any field of science. Good science should be used to answer questions and solve problems, not to do harm.

Second, good science is *peer reviewed*. That means we don't just assume that one person's word is the truth. A trustworthy scientific study is one that is reviewed and validated by independent specialists who have the credentials and experience to make sure the study was done well. Once published in a reputable scientific journal, the study can be scrutinized by even more scientists. By promoting transparency and accountability, peer review keeps good science pointing toward the truth.

Third, good science is *part of a larger body of scientific knowledge*. Every ethical and peer-reviewed scientific study is just one piece of an ever-growing puzzle of knowledge. Just as we cannot rely on a single puzzle piece to show a complete picture, we cannot rely on a single scientific study to provide all the answers. Instead, good science compiles evidence from many different studies that allow us to see the bigger picture and draw stronger conclusions.

Taken together, science can be trusted if it's done ethically, is properly peer reviewed, and is part of a larger body of scientific knowledge.

Science reveals the wonder of God's creation.

Let's take a moment to appreciate the greatness of God's creation as revealed by science.

Here is a question to get us started: Which is the larger number—all of the stars in the Milky Way Galaxy or the number of tiny neural connections in the human mind?

Our mind wins by a longshot. With about 100 billion stars in our Milky Way Galaxy,[8] it would take 1,000 galaxies to approach the number of neural connections in one person's

---

[8] space.com/25959-how-many-stars-are-in-the-milky-way.html

mind.[9] Indeed, we are *"fearfully and wonderfully made"* (Psalm 139:14).

Let's continue on the subject of stars and galaxies. When we look into the night sky without a telescope, we know that nearly every visible star is part of our Milky Way Galaxy. Yet science tells us there is still so much more out there.

The Hubble Telescope is in orbit around the earth, and astronomers recently pointed it at a tiny dark spot in space that had never been explored before. To their surprise, they found 5,500 new galaxies!

In all directions around the telescope, there were millions more dark spots just like the first one. Every time astronomers pointed the telescope at a new spot in space, they found thousands more undiscovered galaxies. Based in part on these discoveries, the latest estimate for the number of galaxies in the universe is *two trillion*.[10]

How many stars are in two trillion galaxies? If we assume that our Milky Way Galaxy has an average number of stars (100 billion), we can estimate the total number of stars in the universe:

---

[9] Drachman, DA. June 2005. "Do we have brain to spare?" Neurology. 64 (12): 2004–5.
[10] forbes.com/sites/startswithabang/2018/10/18/this-is-how-we-know-there-are-two-trillion-galaxies-in-the-universe/#5df9f3025a67

2x10^23, or 200,000,000,000,000,000,000,000 stars.

So, what does this have to do with God? Psalm 147 tells us that God "*determines the number of the stars; he gives to all of them their names. Great is our LORD, and abundant in power; his understanding is beyond measure*" (Psalm 147).

While God's understanding is beyond measure, he continues to use our scientific minds to offer glimpses of his glory. Good science shows us that God's creation is inconceivably big, in terms of stars and galaxies. Good science also reveals that God's creation is astonishingly small. Tiny neural connections in our minds make it possible for us to remember, reason, plan, and do everything else that we do with our minds—including good science.

When we give God the credit for all of creation, our scientific understanding can grow along with our faith. We can also use good science to be better stewards of God's creation.

In Chapter 3, we will focus on what good science tells us about climate change, and we will reflect on how God expects us to respond as stewards.

Jesus said, "I thank you, Father, Lord of heaven and earth, because you have hidden these things from the wise and the intelligent and have revealed them to infants."
\- Matthew 11:25

Prayer Challenge

Let's thank God for creating us with curious minds, and for good science that reveals the wonders of creation.

_____

_____

_____

_____

_____

_____

_____

_____

_____

_____

_____

To add your prayer to the Million Prayer Mission,
please visit MillionPrayerMission.org.

Chapter 3

Good science tells us that God's earth has a fever, and it's getting worse every year.

My daughter wasn't feeling well. I took her temperature, and the thermometer read 99.8 degrees Fahrenheit (°F). She had a minor fever, just over a degree higher than normal. Even so, she went to bed shivering. The poor girl felt so cold that she wore a winter coat and hat to bed under her usual blankets. Later that night, she woke up sweating and feeling too hot. Thankfully, her temperature was back to normal by the next morning, and her wild fever symptoms subsided.

A fever is when our average internal body temperature goes up by more than a degree and stays there for a while. We can usually tell something is wrong because we feel terrible. Like my daughter experienced, a fever of just 1 or 2°F higher than normal can cause all kinds of symptoms: sweating, chills, shivering, headache, body ache, loss of appetite, irritability, dehydration, and/or general weakness.[11]

Although fever symptoms can give us enough to worry about, there are bigger worries to keep in mind. If our fever rises too high, our lives may be in danger. We need to see a doctor. Also, even if our fever is moderate—but it doesn't go back to normal after a few days—then we are still in danger. In that case, we also need to see a doctor.

Can God's earth get a fever?

Yes. Like our bodies, the earth has an equilibrium temperature, and it can overheat.

Earth's equilibrium temperature has remained stable for thousands of years.[12] Since Jesus walked the earth 2,000 years ago, the global average temperature has been about 57°F.[13] That temperature went up and down a little over time, but it stayed within a narrow range. It was almost always about 57°F, plus or minus 1°F.[14]

---

[11] mayoclinic.org/diseases-conditions/fever/symptoms-causes/syc-20352759

[12] climate.gov/news-features/climate-a/what%E2%80%99s-hottest-earth-has-been-%E2%80%9Clately%E2%80%9D

[13] currentresults.com/Environment-Facts/changes-in-earth-temperature.php

[14] ncdc.noaa.gov/global-warming/last-2000-years

Today, the earth's temperature is now 2°F higher than average, and good science tells us that it's going to keep getting hotter. In other words, God's earth has a fever, and it's getting worse.

Because the earth is so big, it has taken decades for the fever to set in. Now that it's here, many of us are experiencing the symptoms:

- record temperatures in air, land, and water
- extreme weather of all kinds
- unmanageable wildfires and smoke
- ocean and freshwater "dead zones"
- ocean acidification
- spreading diseases from mosquitoes, ticks, etc.
- growing risk of animal and plant extinction

Visit climate.nasa.gov/evidence to learn more about climate change and the symptoms of earth's rising fever.

Let's reflect for a moment.

When somebody we care about is sick and they are getting sicker by the day, we pray for them. We know they are in danger, and we ask God to help them.

Would you be willing to pray for your loved ones who depend on God's earth? The earth is sick, it's getting sicker by the day, and we are all in danger.

Consider writing a short prayer here.

_____

_____

_____

_____

_____

The rest of this chapter will summarize the latest science behind climate change. This will be new information for some of us, and for others it will be a review from a different perspective. Either way, you don't need a scientific background to understand this chapter. You do, however, need an open heart and an open mind.

I believe God is calling us to do more than *understand* climate change. He wants us to *own* this problem, pray about it, take action, and encourage others to join us. This is our job as the keepers of God's creation, and it's sacred work.

As you read further, think of ways to make this information your own. Highlight the text and write questions in the margins to look up later. If you feel stuck or confused, take a moment to ask God for help. We all need it.

God's earth has a fever,
and the temperature is only going up.

Our average global temperature has been relatively stable for thousands of years. But this is no longer true. Air, land, and ocean temperatures are increasing faster than ever before in human history.

Figure 1 on the next page shows how much each year's global temperature differs from the 20th-century average (represented by the horizontal line at "0"). The temperature clearly began rising in 1980. Every year since, earth's average temperature has exceeded the 20th-century average, as indicated by the bars rising on the right side of the chart.

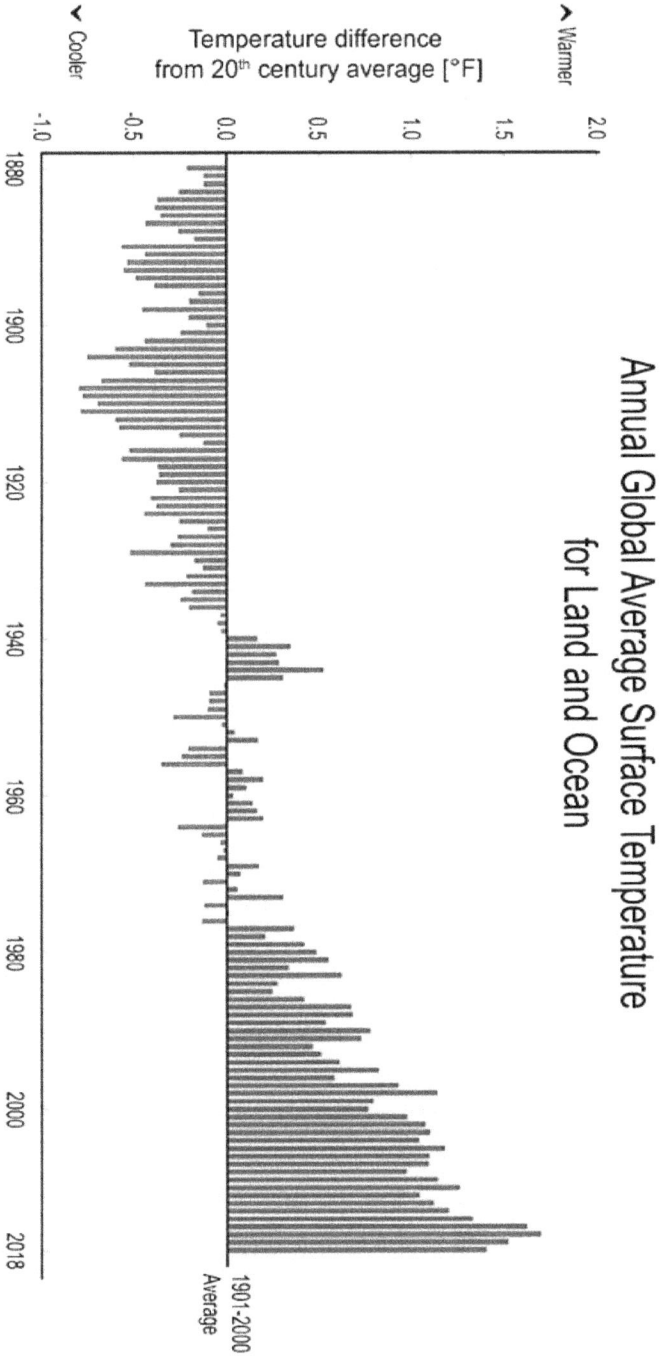

Figure 1 — US Global Change Research Program
www.globalchange.gov/browse/indicators/indicator-global-surface-temperatures

Every year since 1980 has been among the hottest years on record?[15] It's true, and it's shocking. As this book was being written, July 2019 became the hottest month ever recorded,[16] and more records are bound to follow.

As the chart shows, the average global temperature is now 2°F higher than the 20th-century average. Two degrees doesn't sound too bad, right? Wrong.

Let's remember our fever analogy. Even a small change in temperature can mean a big fever. While the symptoms of a fever are painful by themselves, there is even more to be concerned about. If our fever gets too high, then we are in greater danger. Even if our fever is moderate—but our temperature doesn't return to normal—then we are still in danger.

God's earth is facing both scenarios with climate change. First, the global temperature is rising, and it's rising over ten times faster than ever before.[17] Second, unless we do something about it, the earth's temperature will not come back down within this century.

Do we all need to see a doctor yet?

Not everyone is convinced. In the midst of extreme winter

---

[15] climate.nasa.gov/vital-signs/global-temperature/
[16] noaa.gov/news/july-2019-was-hottest-month-on-record-for-planet
[17] earthobservatory.nasa.gov/features/GlobalWarming/page3.php

weather, some people wonder if the earth's temperature is truly rising. Part of the answer is in the story I shared earlier about my daughter's fever: Although her internal body temperature went up, she still felt like she was freezing. Clearly, our bodies respond to excess heat in weird ways. So does the earth. When heat moves up in one direction, it can send cold down in another. In spite of the confusing symptoms, God's earth still has a rising fever.

Unless we do something, the global temperature will keep rising.

To help us understand where the earth's average temperature is going, the US Global Change Research Program assessed different scenarios for the future. Four computer models (RCP2.6, 4.5, 6.0, and 8.5) project a range of possible temperatures over the course of this century. These projections are based on different choices we might make and how the earth is expected to respond. See Figure 2.

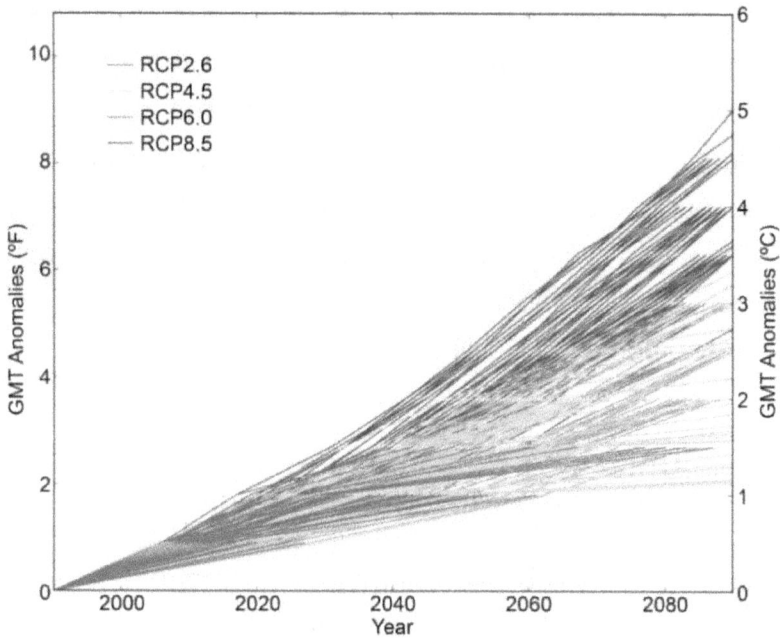

Figure 2 — US Global Change Research Program[18]

Here is the conclusion: In this century, the global temperature could rise between 2° and 9°F higher than it was in the last century.

In many of the scenarios depicted in this chart, the temperature continues to rise as we approach the year 2100. Will we allow it to keep rising?

I used to think that the year 2100 was just the distant future

---

[18] science2017.globalchange.gov/chapter/4

and hardly worth thinking about. But that's no longer the case. In the year 2100, my daughter and son will be in their eighties. Unless we solve climate change, our children, grandchildren, and great-grandchildren will live with the consequences long after we have passed away.

But that's not all. Good science suggests that, if we fail to respond, climate change could impact our descendants for thousands of years.[19]

God created the earth, and God created us. Yet our choices today are threatening both.

Why is the global temperature rising?

In Genesis 1:6-8, God made the atmosphere: *"Let there be a dome in the midst of the waters, and let it separate the waters from the waters…God called the dome Sky."*

The Bible tells us, and science confirms, that our atmosphere is essential to life on earth.

Various gases in our atmosphere act like a greenhouse over the earth by trapping the sun's heat. These gases are appropriately called "greenhouse gases." Without them, the sun's heat would just dissipate into the cold vacuum of space, and our earth would be like a giant snowball.

---

[19] science2017.globalchange.gov/chapter/4

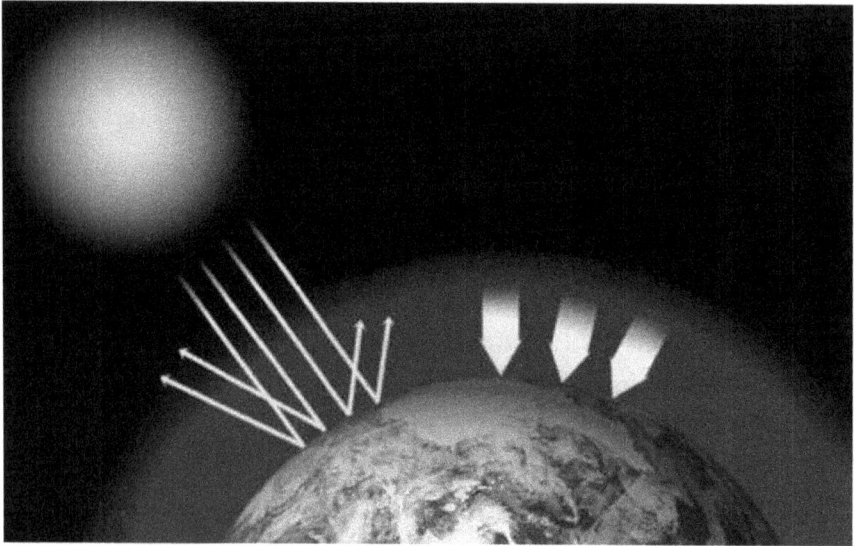

Figure 3 — Credit: NASA

As God intended them, greenhouse gases and the greenhouse effect are actually good things. Unfortunately, too much of a good thing can turn into a bad thing, which is the case with greenhouse gases today. For over a hundred and fifty years, we have been pumping greenhouse gases into the atmosphere at an unprecedented rate. The earth cannot absorb all of our greenhouse gas pollution, so it accumulates in the atmosphere, trapping more and more of the sun's heat. It's as if we are smothering the earth with thick blankets, and we are adding more blankets every year.

We have a runaway greenhouse effect, and that's why God's earth has a runaway fever.

Good Science: US Global Change Research Program

In Chapter 2, we concluded that good science is ethical, peer reviewed, and part of a larger body of scientific knowledge. The United States has its own institution dedicated to good science on climate change, and it's called the US Global Change Research Program.

President George HW Bush established the Program in 1989. Congress then passed a law mandating the Program to "assist the Nation and the world to understand, assess, predict, and respond to human-induced and natural processes of global change" (GlobalChange.gov).

There are thirteen participating federal agencies, including the Department of Commerce, Department of Defense, Department of Energy, Environmental Protection Agency, National Aeronautical and Space Administration, and others. Together with US universities and private institutions, the US Global Change Research Program has been coordinating good science and regular national assessments on climate change for over thirty years.

Thanks to the US Global Change Research Program, the United States has been one of the top funders of, and scientific contributors to, the Intergovernmental

Panel on Climate Change (IPCC, www.ipcc.ch). The IPCC has completed five climate change assessment reports, and a sixth is due in 2022. These reports document an unequivocal consensus: Climate change is real, it's caused by us, it's dangerous, and it will keep getting worse until we solve it.

How do we know that greenhouse gases are increasing in the atmosphere?

In the 1950s, a young man named Dave Keeling was trying to figure out what to do with his life. After earning his doctorate degree, he joined a team that was building a device to measure carbon dioxide (CO_2), the most common greenhouse gas.

Inspired by the possibilities of the device, Dave started measuring airborne CO_2 wherever he went—the California coast, the mountains of Arizona, and the Olympic Peninsula in Washington State. He found that CO_2 was evenly distributed in the atmosphere. His measurements were consistent, about 310 "parts per million" (ppm), as long as he wasn't near a common source of CO_2 pollution, such as a power plant or highway.

Year after year, Dave kept taking measurements, and he discovered that CO_2 levels were increasing. In 1958, his research landed him on the top of a Hawaiian volcano at the

Mauna Loa Observatory. Dave and his colleagues began taking regular measurements of atmospheric CO_2 from Mauna Loa. They did this for decades, and others continue their work today. The result is the "Keeling Curve." It is the longest-running record of direct CO_2 measurements in the world. See Figure 4.

Atmospheric CO_2 at Mauna Loa Observatory

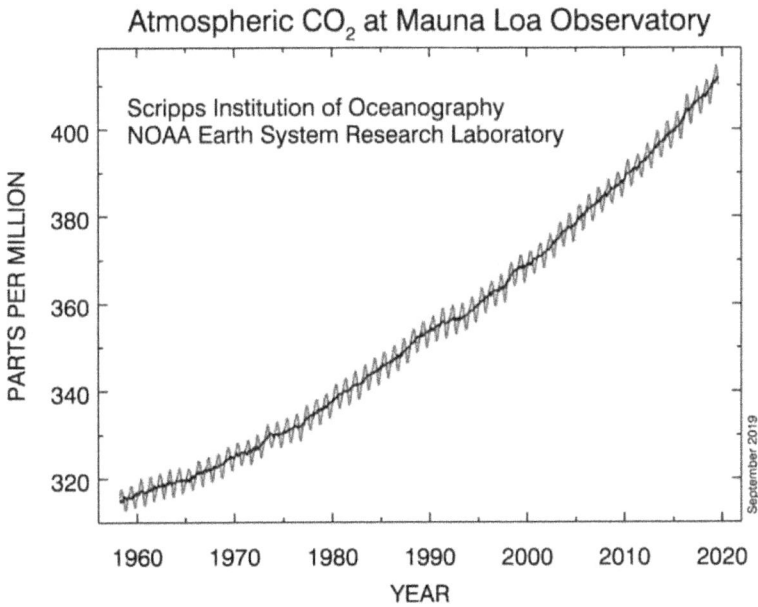

Figure 4 — Scripps Institution of Oceanography and NOAA[20]

Dave Keeling is considered the father of climate change science. Thanks to his discoveries, we learned long ago that

---

[20] esrl.noaa.gov/gmd/webdata/ccgg/trends/co2_data_mlo.png

CO_2 levels were rising every year, and they are still rising.[21] Dave's work inspired scientists to measure the levels of many other greenhouse gases, and they found the same upward trend. These rising levels of greenhouse gases are increasing the earth's average temperature. It's a function of the greenhouse effect.

What did CO_2 concentrations look like before the Keeling Curve began in 1958?

The Keeling Curve is an important piece of the climate change puzzle, but it doesn't show us the CO_2 levels before 1958. We found those missing puzzle pieces deep in the ice sheets of Antarctica and Greenland. Like tree rings, we can count the layers of an ice sheet to determine its age. Using the same layer-counting method, we can tell the age of the air bubbles trapped inside each layer of ice. By drilling deep into ancient ice, scientists have extracted air samples that are up to 800,000 years old.[22] Measuring the CO_2 concentrations of these air samples has given us an accurate CO_2 timeline.

See Figure 5. It shows 400,000 years of CO_2 history. The same pattern actually continues for 800,000 years into the past, but this 400,000-year chart is easier to read.

---

[21] scripps.ucsd.edu/programs/keelingcurve/2013/04/03/the-history-of-the-keeling-curve/

[22] climate.gov/news-features/understanding-climate/climate-change-atmospheric-carbon-dioxide

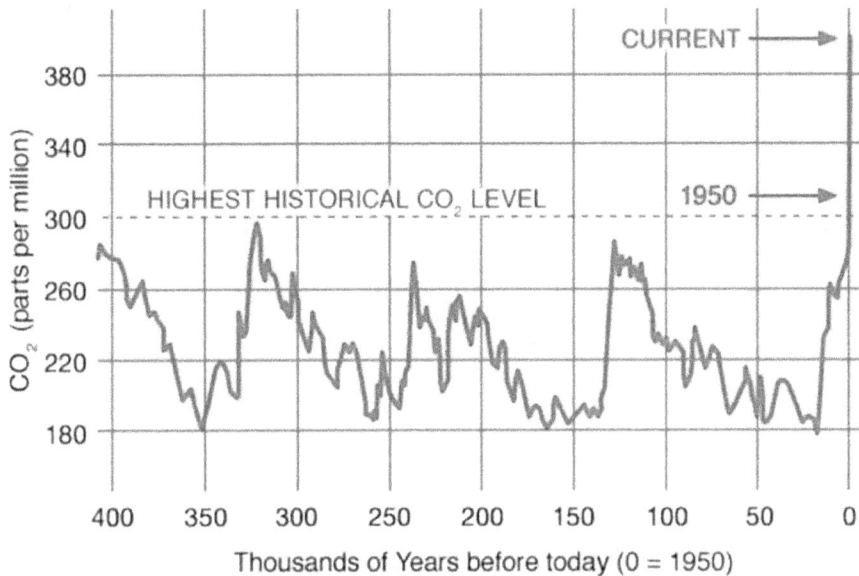

Figure 5 — Credit: NOAA

Here is the chart's main message: Our current CO_2 level (415 ppm and counting) is the highest ever in human history. Every year we break a new record.

Let's take a closer look at the story told by these 400,000 years of CO_2 measurements:

- The vertical axis of the chart shows the concentration of CO_2. The horizontal axis shows thousands of years before 1950.

- Look at the dotted line representing the "highest historical CO_2 level." In 400,000 years, there was never more than 300 ppm of CO_2 in the atmosphere, until 1950. In fact, scientists have doubled the timeline to 800,000 years, and the conclusion is the same.

- Find the "0" mark on the timeline (for the year 1950) and look up at the line showing the increase in CO_2 levels (current). The line is vertical, meaning it's going up fast. From the perspective of 400,000 years, our recent CO_2 increases have happened in the blink of an eye.

- This kind of change is rare on God's good earth, and we have already gone off the chart.

Wait, what are we doing?

Since God created us, there has never been more than 300 ppm of CO_2 in the atmosphere, but today we have 415 ppm.

We depend on a stable climate, and we are not prepared for this much change. It's too much, and it's happening too fast.

To find CO_2 levels as high as today's, we would need to go back *three million* years. Humanity didn't exist yet. The earth was several degrees hotter. Sea levels were fifty to eighty feet higher than they are today.[23]

---

[23] climate.gov/news-features/understanding-climate/climate-change-atmospheric-carbon-dioxide

Is that a world we want to live in, or *can* live in?

God made the earth and saw that it was *"very good."* But if we continue down this destructive path, we will lose the earth that God made for us. In its place will be something foreign and unfamiliar. The earth will not be as good as God intended, and it will no longer point us to our Creator as it once did.

It's time for us to recognize that we have crossed into uncharted and dangerous territory. We need to find our way back home.

*I call heaven and earth to witness against you today
that I have set before you life and death,
blessings and curses.
Choose life so that you and
your descendants may live.*
- Deuteronomy 30:19

Prayer Challenge

Let's ask for God's grace as we absorb this bad news. What is your response as a Christian?

_____

_____

_____

_____

_____

_____

_____

_____

_____

_____

To add your prayer to the Million Prayer Mission,
please visit MillionPrayerMission.org.

Chapter 4

Christians are called to solve climate change, and we need God's help.

On our watch, God's earth has developed a dangerous fever, and our temperature is rising every year.

Climate change hurts all of us. It impacts our air, land, oceans, and communities. It influences storms, floods, heat waves, droughts, wildfires, ocean acidification, rising sea levels, and the spread of diseases.

We are under assault from all sides. Who could be behind all of these problems?

I'm so sorry to say this...but it's me.

And it's also you.

Every one of us contributes to climate change.

Like you, I don't mean to harm God's people or God's earth. So why don't I just stop making climate change worse?

It's partly my weakness of will. Every day, I make choices that cause more greenhouse gas pollution and, therefore, more climate change. In Romans 7:15, Paul reflected on his own weakness: *"I do not understand my own actions. For I do not do what I want, but I do the very thing I hate."* That's how I feel as I continue to pollute, even though I know better.

While I'm responsible for my own pollution, I'm not an island. Society influences my choices and yours. Many of the reasons that I pollute are the same reasons that you pollute, so we are in this together.

Here are some of the major sources of my greenhouse gas pollution.

Carbon dioxide (CO_2) is my most common greenhouse gas pollutant. When I burn fossil fuels—such as gasoline, natural gas, oil, or coal—I release carbon dioxide into the atmosphere as a byproduct. I make climate change worse when I drive or ride in a fossil-fuel-powered vehicle or when I fly in a fossil-fuel-powered airplane. Because some of my electricity is generated by burning fossil fuels, I make climate change worse when I use that electricity to power my lights, appliances, computer, smart phone, and many other devices at home and work.

Methane (CH4), or natural gas, is my second-most common greenhouse gas pollutant. It can trap over thirty times more heat than carbon dioxide. The production of fossil fuels, which I use, results in methane pollution. Closer to home, when the natural gas pipeline connected to my house springs a leak, that methane rises into the atmosphere and makes climate change worse. Even when I send yard waste or food waste to the landfill, it can break down to produce landfill methane pollution. Those are just a few examples of my methane pollution sources.

My least common pollutants are called *high global warming potential (high-GWP) greenhouse gases.* They are powerful and long-lasting in the atmosphere. They include N2O, CFCs, HFCs, HCFCs, PFCs, and SF6.[24] Some of these gases are used to manufacture everyday products, such as my refrigerator and air conditioner. Some are anesthetic gases that doctors have used on me for surgery (while venting the excess gas out the hospital's exhaust pipe and into the atmosphere). There are many uses of these potent gases, but their consequences are dramatic. Once in the atmosphere, they trap heat at a rate of hundreds to thousands of times more than carbon dioxide traps heat. They can also stay in the atmosphere for hundreds or thousands of years.

---

[24] epa.gov/ghgemissions/understanding-global-warming-potentials

Pollution is a sin.

Let's face it. My greenhouse gas pollution is wrong. It's making climate change worse, and it's hurting God's people and God's earth. That offends God.

There is a Biblical word for any action, or inaction, that hurts others and offends God. The word is "sin."

My sin presents me with a few choices.

- Do nothing (and continue to sin).
- Ask for forgiveness but change nothing (and continue to sin).
- Ask for forgiveness and change everything that I can.

As a Christian, and as a parent, I choose option three.

Making this choice is only the first step. Overcoming my sin will not be easy, and I am bound to make mistakes along the way.

Even the disciples failed when Jesus needed them most. On the night before giving his life for all of us on the cross, Jesus found his disciples sleeping instead of doing what he had asked—praying.

Jesus challenged them, and he challenges us now, to *"stay awake and pray that you may not come into the time of trial; the spirit indeed is willing, but the flesh is weak"* (Matthew 26:41).

For climate change, our time of trial has arrived. It's time for us to wake up and pray.

What does the Bible say about climate change?

The Gospel books of Matthew, Mark, Luke, and John tell the stories of Jesus' life and teachings in over 64,000 words. Not surprisingly, the words "climate change" cannot be found among them. That's because the Gospels were not written to address every possible problem by name. Instead, Jesus gave us principles of faith (what to believe) and principles of ethics (what to do).

Biblical principles can apply to any problem, so let's consider how they apply to climate change.

Love God.

As we discussed in Chapter 2, Jesus was once asked to name the first of God's commandments. He responded: *"The first is, 'Hear, O Israel: the Lord our God, the Lord is one; you shall love the Lord your God with all your heart, and with all your soul, and with all your mind, and with all your strength'"* (Mark 12:29-30).

There are two ways to express our love for God: prayer and action.

Jesus placed great value on prayer. He prayed often, and he

taught us to do the same. At the same time, Jesus made it clear that he expects more than prayers alone. He also wants to see action. *"Not everyone who says to me, 'Lord, Lord,' will enter the kingdom of heaven, but only the one who does the will of my Father in heaven"* (Matthew 7:21).

We can express our love for God by praying and acting to protect his people and his earth from runaway climate change.

Love your neighbor.

After referring first to the commandment to love God, Jesus added a second commandment: *"You shall love your neighbor as yourself"* (Mark 12:31).

And who is our neighbor? In the Parable of the Good Samaritan, Jesus explained that our neighbor is anyone in need, regardless of their status. After other people ignored an injured man on the side of a road, only the Samaritan took notice and took care of him. The injured man was from a different and rival culture, so normally the two men would not have even spoken to one another. But the Samaritan treated the injured man like a brother anyway. Jesus concludes the story with these words: *"Go and do likewise"* (Luke 10:37).

Again, Jesus wants to see action. He calls us to *"go and do."* He also instructs us to *"Do to others as you would have them do to you"* (Luke 6:31). This is the famous Golden Rule, and it begins with a verb.

How does Jesus' commandment to love our neighbor apply to climate change? It's simple: Everyone who is in need is our neighbor, and everyone is threatened by climate change.

Love the least of these.

After defining our neighbor as everyone in need, Jesus challenges us to think especially of the less fortunate. *"Truly I tell you, just as you did it to one of the least of these who are members of my family, you did it to me"* (Matthew 25:31-46).

Throughout his ministry, Jesus focused on people who were poor, sick, marginalized, powerless, and vulnerable. These are the *"least of these."* By definition, they are at risk, and they are the people hurt most by climate change. The poor don't have extra resources to recover from storms, floods, droughts, and wildfires. If Jesus cares about their lives, so should we.

Love the children.

Among the least of these, Jesus considered children a special group. He even rebuked his disciples when they tried to keep children away: *"Let the little children come to me; do not stop them; for it is to such as these that the kingdom of God belongs"* (Mark 10:14).

Do we believe Jesus when he tells us that the kingdom of God belongs to children? If so, we need to ask ourselves: Is our greenhouse gas pollution keeping our children from experiencing God's kingdom here on earth?

Unless we solve climate change, today's children and generations of unborn children will inherit a dangerous planet that hardly resembles the one God created for them.

In summary, Jesus calls us to love God by loving our neighbor, the poor, and children. We can love them all by praying and acting to solve climate change.

Why should Christians care about this earth if it's only going to pass away in the end?

Many Christians believe that Jesus will come again to renew the earth and establish God's kingdom (2 Peter 3:8-13, Revelation 21).

However, we don't know all of the specifics of this prophecy. First, we don't know exactly *how* it will happen. Second, we don't know *when* it will happen, which is why Peter wrote, *"...with the Lord one day is like a thousand years, and a thousand years are like one day"* (2 Peter 3:8).

If God's earth will one day pass away, then does that mean we have a free pass to harm the earth? Of course not. God created it, and the earth belongs to God.

The same rule applies to people. Each of God's people will eventually pass away from this world. Does that mean we have a free pass to hurt people? Of course not. God created each of us in his image and likeness. We each belong to God.

To be good Christians, we don't need to know how or when Jesus will renew the earth. We just need to act on what we already know: *"The earth is the LORD's and all that is in it, the world, and those who live in it"* (Psalm 24:1). We will be held accountable for the way we treat God's people and God's earth. Jesus makes that clear in the Gospels.

As the keepers of God's creation, we are called to protect and restore the earth for everyone's benefit. If we take that responsibility seriously, then I believe God will use us to renew his earth and establish his kingdom.

We need Christ's courage.

Before we take on our climate crisis, let's take a sober look at the work ahead of us.

Solving climate change will not be cheap or easy. For Christians, that is no surprise because Jesus never promised us a cheap or easy life. Instead, he showed us how to love fearlessly and without counting the cost. He showed us the way of the cross.

In John 16:33, our Savior proclaimed, *"In the world you face persecution. But take courage; I have conquered the world!"*

Today, we need Christ's courage to stand up to a worldly addiction. Addiction is marked by continuing to use a substance even though we know it's harmful, and this is exactly the situation we're in with cheap and easy fossil fuels. Our greenhouse gas pollution from burning fossil fuels is harming God's people and God's earth. Unless we push back against our addiction, society will continue telling us: *Just keep using fossil fuels, and don't worry about the consequences.*

For over one hundred and fifty years, fossil fuels have been an important source of profit and power around the world, and that is still the case. To be fair, fossil energy has provided us countless benefits. But now we know better. Why would we continue to pursue profit and power at the expense of God's people and God's earth?

Jesus said, *"If any want to become my followers, let them deny themselves and take up their cross and follow me...For what will it profit them if they gain the whole world but forfeit their life? Or what will they give in return for their life? For the Son of Man is to come with his angels in the glory of his Father, and then he will repay everyone for what has been done"* (Matthew 16: 25-27).

Jesus also said, *"No one can serve two masters...You cannot serve God and wealth"* (Matthew 6:24).

As Christians, we are not bound by the fossil fuel economy. We are free to break our addiction and find a better way to live. We know that meaningful change will not be cheap or easy. It never is. But in the end, it will be much less costly than the self-destructive path we are on now.

We need God.

Climate change is a big and complex problem. Over the past few decades, some of the smartest people in the world have been unable to solve it. It's bigger than you, me, or any other individual. It's also bigger than any organization, corporation, or government in the world.

To tackle climate change, we need to work more closely together than ever before, and at every level. Solving climate change requires global cooperation in science, technology, law, finance, and more. We need commitments and accountability from every nation. Most importantly, we need local investment and action to cut our greenhouse gas pollution.

This is the greatest collective-action challenge in human history.

Sadly, instead of working together, we just keep falling into the same trap. It's called the "tragedy of the commons." That is, while everyone is partially responsible for climate change, nobody is willing to take full responsibility. It seems too costly to act alone, or even to go first. It's easier to point the finger at others and say, "You polluted more than we did..." or "You have more money than we do, so you need to change first." The result is predictable: We all keep polluting, and climate change keeps getting worse.

To state the obvious, climate change is a massive mess, and

the mess just keeps growing. After more than thirty years of trying, we haven't been able to clean it up.

How, then, can Christians possibly help to solve climate change?

We can begin by looking at the problem differently. This is not just another man-made problem in search of a man-made solution. Climate change now threatens all of God's people and all of God's earth. It has grown into a God-sized problem, and we need a God-sized solution.

We need a miracle.

We need a Savior.

We need God.

I lift up my eyes to the hills—
from where will my help come?
My help comes from the LORD,
who made heaven and earth.
- Psalm 121

Prayer Challenge

Have you ever made such a big mess that you couldn't clean it up by yourself? To whom did you turn for help?

Will you ask for God's help with our climate change mess?

_____

_____

_____

_____

_____

_____

_____

_____

_____

To add your prayer to the Million Prayer Mission,
please visit MillionPrayerMission.org

Chapter 5

Let's pray, act, and pray again.

We need God's help to solve climate change.

So what does it look like to rely on God in a time of great need? For a good example, let's reflect on a Gospel story...

One evening, as the sun was setting, the disciples of Jesus were trying to cross the Sea of Galilee in a little boat. Unfortunately, they sailed straight into a storm. The wind and waves turned against them, and the disciples ended up fighting the elements into the night.

Exhausted, helpless, and far from shore, they suddenly saw a man walking toward them. He was walking on the water!

At first, they thought it was a ghost. Then the man said, *"Take heart, it is I; do not be afraid."*

They knew that voice. It was Jesus.

Peter answered him, "Lord, if it is you, command me to come to you on the water." He said, "Come." So Peter got out of the boat, started walking on the water, and went toward Jesus.

But when he noticed the strong wind, he became frightened, and beginning to sink, he cried out, "Lord, save me!" Jesus immediately reached out his hand and caught him, saying to him, "You of little faith, why did you doubt?"

When they got into the boat, the wind ceased. And those in the boat worshiped Jesus, saying, "Truly You are the Son of God" (Matthew 14:26-33).

Peter gives us a model to follow: pray, act, and pray again.

When he and his fellow disciples were in need, Peter called out to Jesus for help. It was a prayer, although in this case it was face-to-face.

Knowing that Jesus was with him gave Peter the courage to act. Despite the wind and waves, he quickly got out of the boat and started walking on the water toward Jesus.

It was a moment that must have taken Peter's breath away. He walked on water! Imagine the look on his face. It was a miracle, and it was a result of both prayer and action.

But then Peter noticed the strong wind. Suddenly his fear overcame his faith. He started to doubt, and he started to sink. That's when Peter cried out again for help, *"Lord, save me!"*

It was a second prayer. Jesus caught him, and the wind stopped.

Solving our climate crisis is like crossing the Sea of Galilee.

In a sense, we are all trying to cross the Sea of Galilee in a little boat. The winds and waves of climate change are only getting stronger. How should we respond as Christians?

Will we remember that Jesus is with us and ready to help? Like Peter, are we ready to pray for that help? Are we then willing to act? And when our actions fall short, will we pray again?

If we wish to solve climate change, then we need to pray, act, and pray again. Why? Because God's kingdom is on the move when our prayers lead to actions, and our actions lead to more prayers. Our spiritual momentum grows.

What will it look like when God comes to our rescue? Maybe he will inspire millions of people to pray for the first time. Maybe he will empower each of us to act beyond our natural abilities. Maybe, in response to our faith, he will work wonders beyond anything we can imagine.

If the Bible is any indication, God is ready to do all of the above.

Will you join the Million Prayer Mission?

The Million Prayer Mission is a global relay race to solve climate change, and our prayers are doing the racing. Here's how it works:

Step 1: Pray. Visit MillionPrayerMission.org to say "amen" to a pre-written prayer. Or you can write your own. Your prayer can be as short as a word, or it can be longer. If you're feeling more creative, then your prayer can include a link to a photo, video, song, or other online content. Your prayer can be anonymous, or you can include your name. Feel free to return and post as many prayers as you wish.

Step 2: Pass it on. Jesus said, *"Where two or three are gathered in my name, I am there among them"* (Matthew 18:20). Would you be willing to invite two or three people to join the Million Prayer Mission? Simply share the link (MillionPrayerMission.org) and ask if they would be willing to post a prayer within two weeks.

Remember the power of *two*. If we all invite at least *two* people to post a prayer within *two* weeks, and they each do the same, we could reach a million prayers within *two* years! That is the potential of exponential prayer.

Think of your prayer as a beam of light. Every time you pray and invite others to pray, God's light shines from you to them. With every new person who joins the Million Prayer Mission, the light multiplies—radiating in every direction—connecting people across cities, states, nations, and continents. Eventually, our prayers will circle the earth, and they will just keep going.

This is an opportunity to be the *"light of the world"* that Jesus calls us to be.

Nothing is impossible for God.

This book began with the Parable of the Mustard Seed, and we will close with it too.

Jesus said, *"Truly I tell you, if you have faith as small as a mustard seed, you can say to this mountain, 'Move from here to there,' and it will move. Nothing will be impossible for you"* (Matthew 17:20).

Like a mountain, climate change can sometimes appear impossible to move. That's why we, as Christians, turn to God with our faith and prayers. While our prayers may seem small to us, God sees them differently.

With great hope and anticipation, we ask: What will God do with our million mustard seeds? What will he do with our million prayers?

I believe God will answer our prayers. I believe he will help us to solve our climate crisis by working a million miracles in our hearts, homes, churches, and communities.

In doing so, God will advance his kingdom—*"on earth as it is in heaven"* (Matthew 6:10).

Will you pray with me?

Our Father in heaven,
hallowed be your name.
Your kingdom come.
Your will be done,
on earth as it is in heaven.
Give us this day our daily bread.
And forgive us our debts,
as we also have forgiven our debtors.
And do not bring us to the time of trial,
but rescue us from evil.
- Matthew 6:9-13

Prayer Challenge

Consider how you can help to solve climate change at a local level—in your own home, church, and community. Whom will you ask to join you?

What would it look like to *pray, act, and pray again* until God creates a breakthrough moment?

_____

_____

_____

_____

_____

_____

_____

_____

_____

To add your prayer to the Million Prayer Mission,
please visit MillionPrayerMission.org

A MILLION PRAYERS

TO SOLVE OUR CLIMATE CRISIS

Acknowledgments

Anna, you are the love of my life. Thank you for encouraging me in faith. For some reason, God put this book on my heart within a month after Sam was born. We were never so short on time and energy, and still you supported me. Thank you for taking care of Sam and Rachel while I wrote. Thank you for making each chapter better with your thoughtful review and advice. I could not have written this book without you.

Rachel, you are the best daughter in the world. At age five, you told me, "Even if you think it's the end, it's never the end with God." You also asked, "Dad, do you know that if God is with you, you're never really alone?" Thank you for reminding me of God's boundless love and presence. Never forget that you are made in the image and likeness of God. I love you, I am so proud of you, and I have faith in you.

Sam, you are the best son in the world. When you opened your eyes and looked into mine for the first time, I knew I had to write this book. I wrote it while you were a baby, with the hope you and Rachel would one day experience the restoration of God's creation. You both have important roles to play in that great work. Thank you for inspiring me. I love you, I am so proud of you, and I have faith in you.

Mom and Dad, I cannot thank you enough. Now that I'm a parent myself, I know how much you gave, and continue to give, to your children. Thank you for your love, time, and support. Thank you for showing me, Matt, and Danny the beauty and adventure of God's creation. Most of all, thank you for giving us the gift of faith.

Grandma Bettye and Grandpa Chuck, Grandma Muriel and Grandpa Gene: Thank you for your love, hospitality, and generosity; for all the good memories and life lessons; for your faith and prayers on behalf of your grandchildren; and for the inspiring roles you played in the Greatest Generation. May our generation live up to your example.

Chris Bentley, you always make a point to address me as *my friend*. Thank you for being a steadfast friend, advisor, chief information officer, and partner in launching the Million Prayer Mission.

Shelley Allen of Ruthless Red Pen, thank you for your kindness, professionalism, and prayers, as well as your tireless editing and formatting. Stephen Howard of The Editing Bard, thanks for your developmental editing, thoughtful advice, referrals, and encouragement to help me begin the process of transforming the manuscript into a book. Thanks also to Frank Ball for assisting with the cover design, chapter icons, and website graphics.

Georgetown University, Dahlgren Chapel, and Saint Thomas Apostle Catholic Church in Washington, DC; Saint Bernard of Clairvaux Catholic Church and Saint Patrick Catholic Community in Scottsdale, Arizona. Thank you for laying a strong foundation.

Pastor Mark Batterson and National Community Church: Your "brave" has been my breakthrough. I attended the original

Theater Church in the basement of Union Station (popcorn in church!), and I will never forget the casual freedom of my first service at Ebenezers Coffeehouse. Although I moved away from DC, I continued to listen to NCC podcasts. I also read *In a Pit with a Lion on a Snowy Day*, *Chase the Lion*, *Whisper*, and *The Circle Maker*. In fact, *The Circle Maker* inspired the Million Prayer Mission, which is the biggest prayer circle that I could imagine. Thank you for enriching my faith with your enthusiastic prayers and courageous actions. This book affirms, as you do, that "every -ology is a form of theology" and "God is bigger than our biggest problems."

Pastor Jesse Whitford and Baker City Christian Church: You loaned me *The Circle Maker*. You walked and prayed with me. You challenged me, perhaps more than you know, to write this book. Thank you.

Author's Note

This book is a prayer...for a million prayers.

Who am I to ask for a million prayers? My qualifications are simple: I'm a Christ-follower, and I'm a parent. Through a combination of prayer, research, and reason, I have concluded that loving God and loving my family means taking climate change seriously.

In the spirit of Ephesians 2:8-10, I can't really take credit for this book. It's my response to a sense of calling that I can only attribute to God's grace—the kind of grace that loves and calls even a sinner like me. Therefore, God gets the credit for anything that is good and true within these pages, while I take responsibility for any omissions or errors.

I have been blessed with the support of many generous people along this journey. You, the reader, are among them. Thank you for taking the time to read and pray with me.

Do you believe that God is bigger than climate change? Do you believe in the power of prayer? If so, please visit MillionPrayerMission.org to join other Christians who have committed to pray and act to help solve our climate crisis.

May God give all of us faith to pray and courage to act.

Peter Fargo

Have you not known? Have you not heard?
The LORD is the everlasting God,
the Creator of the ends of the earth.
He does not faint or grow weary;
his understanding is unsearchable.
He gives power to the faint,
and strengthens the powerless.
Even youths will faint and be weary,
and the young will fall exhausted;
but those who wait for the LORD
shall renew their strength,
they shall mount up with wings like eagles,
they shall run and not be weary,
they shall walk and not faint.
- Isaiah 40:28-31

www.ingramcontent.com/pod-product-compliance
Lightning Source LLC
Chambersburg PA
CBHW061154040426
42445CB00013B/1678